False Starts
and Mishaps

A Book of Poetry, Aphorisms,
and a Short Story

Daniel Bates, LMHC

DB PRESS
Creative Endeavors That Matter

ISBN: 0997311568
ISBN 13: 978-0997311563
Library of Congress Control Number: 2016911262
DB PRESS, Vancouver Washington

Dedicated to Emily Dickinson.

Table of Contents

Introduction

Creativity is not about formulating the perfect idea. It's about formulating enough ideas till you find a winner.

Do you agree or disagree?

I can understand skepticism regarding this idea. It makes sense that in order to come up with a really great idea you have to put a great deal of work into it. Therefore, instead of spreading yourself thin, concentrate all your efforts into project. On the surface, this idea looks like common sense, but this is where common sense fails you. Creativity is not intuitive, it's counter-intuitive. Let me explain why.

There is more trial and error in creativity than you may realize. I once heard an analogy that may shed light on this point. In a college pottery class a professor split the class into two groups. Each group was given the same assignment: to make the best vase over the course of 1 month. However, each group had to obey different rules. Group 1 could use as much time as they wanted on each vase they created. Group 2 could only spend a limited amount of time on each vase.

After the month elapsed the professor had the two groups present their final work. Each group, after a lot of hard work, unveiled their final product. It was assumed by many in the class that group 1 had an unfair advantage and was more likely to win.

Given the limitations of Group 2 and the advantage of Group 1 you can see why they thought this. However, to everyone's shock, the two vases unveiled could not have been more different. The quality, aesthetics, and sturdiness were demonstrably evident.

Group 2's vase was unparalleled in every way. Most agreed if not all agreed that group 2's vase was superior to Group 1. But how could this be? Group 1 didn't have any constraints. At best, Group 2 was slated to produce more, but no one thought their product would be better.

The class demanded an answer from the professor. The professor smiled. He explained that because Group 2 was forced to produce more, they were given greater opportunity to learn from their mistakes. This allowed them to reflect, make modifications and ultimately create a beautiful final product whereas Group 1 put an inordinate amount of time into only a few vases effectively limiting their mistakes and limiting their learning. Therefore, more vases lead to more mistakes which lead to more learning and eventually to a better product.

The lesson for creative types, writers, and poets— and anyone really—write a lot and make a lot of mistakes. Don't get hung up on making your work perfect. And don't give up. The first book I wrote was an abysmal failure. The writing wasn't good. The structure of the book was nonexistent. My sentences were clunky and unclear. I didn't know who my target audience was. I probably made every writing mistake you could make. And sadly, I spent 2 ½ years on the thing.

I could have looked at all those failures and given up on my dream of becoming a writer and poet. But, instead I learned from my mistakes and kept writing. I realized the first book was exactly that, my first. It wasn't my one and only shot at writing a book I could be proud of. And the book wasn't my one and only good idea either. It was, in fact, the gatekeeper to a host of future ideas and books. After making this realization, I found that I was more excited to write. I had more ideas. I was more passionate and better equipped to execute new projects.

I now see my past writing failures as essential to my current writing successes. This same concept applies to poetry. When I first started writing poetry my work wasn't good. It was very touchy-feely, autobiographical, more of a journal. But over the course of my 1000 by 30 project I've discovered my voice. I found that I have something to say. And the devices and conventions of poetry enhanced my voice. Poetic devices deepened the meaning of what I was trying to say. Unfortunately, I didn't reach my goal of writing 1000 poems by the time I turned 30. I'm 30 and have roughly written 500 poems. But I'm not disappointed. The 1000 poems goal was an arbitrary number. The intent was to force me to be creative when there are so many demands upon my attention and time. And I'm glad I did it.

My challenge to you, force yourself to create even when you don't feel like it. Simply showing up is enough. Don't relegate your need for creativity to the back burner. Also, embrace the process of failure. Trust that your mistakes will lead to success. Trust that your current idea that feels like a dud will lead a stroke of genius. That dud will be a stepping stone to your magnum opus. And finally, keep in mind it is an act of courage to create. Don't think for a second that it's trivial. No one else can articulate your vision with your voice and your passion. Only you can breathe life into your idea.

Section 1: Poetry

The Mission of Art

Art is going deeper than you've

Ever gone before.

It's about saying everything,

And then saying even more.

Its inspiration happening when

Everything goes wrong

You reflect, you see what

Got you through.

Then share the story.

Realize your strength,

The strength that lies

In all of us.

Your story then draws it out,

Of the rest of us.

Your story, the art,

Makes us all better.

You redeem the irredeemable,

And then pass it on to the rest.

Waiting

Between the known and unknown

As one watches their loved

One lay on bed of questions

As one waits for news

From doctor or scan or procedure.

Lulls and highs and a lot

Of tense waiting.

The news won't change

Could good or bad

But it won't ever change

It always and immutably is

Is the life change you feared

Or confirmation of status quo

But it will never change

No matter the planning and

Worrying; it won't change

Must, should, and imperative it is

That you wait in between

Witnesses and Guardians

Witnesses standing before a
Mausoleum of human tragedy

People encircle, crestfallen
Like apparitions

Guardians who failed and
Couldn't protect

Whose role now is
Picking up broken pieces

The pieces of a person
Left behind by destructive events

Witnesses watching- surreal-
The darker side of humanity? No

This is humanity. It is dark
It is a mother wailing

A Son blaming himself
A father silently weeping

Dumb, foolish kids
Using a gun to solve a fight

So the guardians stand
Encircling, keeping out eyes

Powerless to prevent, only to
Stand and watch

Only to serve, once the worst
Has happened

Only to listen to hypotheticals like
" Only if…" and "If only…."

The tools to save
Don't always work

And only is there to do
Stand, watch and witness

Three Steps to Write a Poem

1. Sit down (somewhere alone)
2. Find a feeling (doesn't have to be your own)
3. Hide inside your words (they allow you to be shown)

Reframing

We hang frames on events

Constructed with words and ideas

Internal constructs that shape

That mold, that bend like hot metal,

The externalities of our lives.

Below and beneath are skyscrapers

Scaffolding upon scaffolding

Like the tower of Babel

Extending to the upper reaches of consciousness

Made of nails to hang our frames

Some big, some small

Growing and diminishing with time

The events unchanging and

The frame yet in flux

For the fiber of a frame

The scaffolding and its struts

Can change and be altered

Depending on the lux

For light shows a picture

That is bigger than our own

It illuminates truth

And makes the unknown known

To reframe a negative interpretation

Reveals you are not alone

Because your assumption made you bitter

A bitter wall that cuts you off

From others and your dreams

At compassion you scoff

But to see the hurt and noble within

Connects you to other like a safety pin

Acting a reentrance to community

By loving the unlovable in unity

By seeing a new meaning in the story

Instead of seeing solely pain and the gory

Once Forgotten Truth

Life repeats in message and tone

We learn nothing new, but how

The why is debated, the perspectives are old

Like the nine maidens endow

Endless imagination of a once forgotten truth

The residue sticks on our minds

And rests in our souls

Hiding and popping out

In response to its antithetic

My Pit

The pit I am in, locked with key

Not of metal, but fashioned of flesh

Accessed by in-breaking of song

A song of echoes

Of past peoples and places

That touched and molded

Of hurts and wounds

Mournfully playing in my pit

Will you crawl in?

Will you sing my song?

With Jeremiah and Jesus

As they lamented over Jerusalem

As Hannibal watching over Carthage

Will you be my crèche?

Opening my pit with key of flesh?

Fashioned by song and empathy

Looking upon me with clemency

Alone

Riding along the way to my home street

Shoulders, elbows, knees

Bumping together like low hanging trees

Arriving at the street, crowds I must fight

Getting to a place for me means no delight

A home I felt surrounded by strangers

In whose walls are countless dangers

Killing Jesus in his manger

Was a man who spewed hate with a hug

Refused responsibility like a drug

The room, again crowded with stares and forlorn

Present for support, internally torn

Ambivalent they are of what is to come

Anxious to avoid, the death beat drum

More necks, and colors of dandruff

Encouraging me to be tough

Back to the way I go

Into the endless people flow

Passing like a ghostly glow

Inquisitor of Hypocrisy

Struggling to follow my own rules

Feeling the fool, victim of my own hands

One and two and three and four

How many times must I ignore

Before I'm rocked to the core

Addiction's Combat

Sitting between two trucks, smoking a cigarette

Staring at buildings bearing my regret

The sun soothes sorrows of a lifetime

Small pleasures provide some sublime

Sunbeams as clear as memories

My son on my knees, youthful reveries

Beams on my neck where my daughter sat

Losing her to addiction's brutal combat

Kids gone and I was wrong for what I did

I've been sliding through life's long skid

On the slow roll

The eeking stroll

Down the broad path of destruction

Along the winding mysterious fluxion

And no comfort are these skies

Little joy I gather from sunbeams and memories

As I sit between two trucks, smoking a cigarette

Starting at buildings bearing my regret

A Poem to Disregard

Of life and love and all its vain importance

Of men and money and all its discordance

Where do we go with no guidance?

Who do we turn casting off manners and countenance?

When we shed our masks and bear our souls

When we cleave a modicum of control

And come to the one who can make us whole

Yes, a poem about God easy to disregard

The mention causing you to put up guard

But consider for a moment

Life and its big picture

Of its purpose and its stricture

Of where you fit

And who you are

What gives you meaning?

And who do you inspire?

The Dragon

Chasing a moment

A flight of whimsy

When we really

See beyond

All that can be

Physically perceived

Meditation on Men and Anger

Men are angry animals

Brimming like hot kettles

Waiting, hoping to boil

Wanting the steam

Wanting an excuse to boil

Ever watchful and on the hunt

For an ignition point

To take the brunt

Pressure and heat

Violently meet

And let the man

Work out his feelings

All mixed up and complex

But anger is a clearinghouse

An organizing force at best

Putting head on straight

For the man

Letting him exhaust

Pent up mental spam

At worst, a scene

Messier than it was

An animal not a man

A base feeling

No access to the rest

For anger is a key

And not a test

Listen to the anger

And unlock the man

Not the animal

A Family Who Must

Death mostly hoary

Ghastly and gory

Of a foot ending

A bed

Of a dad

Pathetic and dead

Matriarch come to choose

Try and die

Stop and lose

The man is dead

Either way

A family now

Who must face

The day

Parts

At war with me

Inside of me

Fighting for

What was

Who I am

Is what I do

And not because

The past has set

It always is

A changing pictograph

God Bows

Fantasy to see

At videos touch

Fact and fiction

At confliction

For thoughts materialize

Before your eyes

Putting man in God's seat

To man's feet

God bows

Because man makes

And creates

His dark dream

From a machine

Forcing God's knee

Fall like a key

A Woman Across the Way

When can a man see her,

the woman across the

way. A woman great in

beauty. Only she will

Say.

Baby Laila

Sweet dreams baby Laila

May you sleep like a bird

Amongst soft nest, of love

May you sleep like bunnies

Snuggled snuggly below

In home defended by mom

And made by daddy

A home of warmth

That won't make you batty

So sleep Laila baby

For you are loved my star

Sing Angels

Sing angels to my sweet.

Sing angels, don't miss a beat.

Sing to my daughter,

That she may sleep.

She, God's gift to me.

She makes me whole and complete.

Sing Angels so I don't despair

And dwell too long

Upon my failings and lack.

Upon my human limited care

To her needs and growth.

Tethered I am to the human condition.

My daughter, I don't

Want to make a rendition

Of where I fall short

And all my mistakes.

Her life, of the highest stakes.

So sing Angels to my despair.

Sing Angels for my heir.

Of Trains and Men

Tracks of train rumble in the distance,

Echoing my heart's discontent.

A train passes through the night,

And I struggle with struggling.

The lanes change seldomly

I'm sick of the same ol' battling.

Can a train change his ways?

Or is the train stuck on one track?

Is a man the same?

A man unchanged all his days?

Life Rich Internal

The ravages of life it seems

Can suck a life right out.

The joy maim by hardship,

Pleasures out of reach.

Succumb or bitter, choose,

Not many options present.

Yet a life rich internal,

Leads to betterment.

A life of mind, soul

Propped up by imagining.

Despite the toil and despair.

Despite loss, little love to spare

A life as brutal as this,

Only coped by awe and whim,

Of thought, love and hymn.

Unfading Sun

Let loss be your guide,

Down a path of dim candlelight.

Steps appear and vanish,

Like high school Spanish.

You must walk a lonely road;

Missing the sense of complete.

Half are you without them,

Like a bed with no sheet.

Pregnant are the steps,

With loss and memory.

But the road becomes bearable,

Yet wounds undeniable.

But your steps, one by one,

Will land firmly in their place.

In the spirit of the one you loved,

Like an unfading cavalcade.

Recompense

Blessed are you that recompense.

Who say sorry when wrong,

And make steps of amends.

For words are precursors to action

And do not act as distraction.

They are not placeholders for contrition.

You must do as you say,

And put away foolish play.

For the there will be a day,

When you are wronged

And not easily calmed

You'll demand torture prolonged

Of the offender,

Regardless of the gender.

You'll want their head in a blender.

So be blessed instead,

I say to you,

And make recompense.

Holding Another's Pain

Blessed be the one

Who holds another's pain

Who stands where others walk away

Who sits when others pacing in disdain

Who opens when others close their hearts

To lend an ear and not a loudly shared opinion

You who give life by sharing their own

Who gladly offer hearts at homes

By making space for others

You are blessed for you

Go and Bless others

Teeter Totter

Delicate, but true

Always presents a taboo

To err and

Be too nice too

Concise with an evaluation

Of the other

Balance is a challenge

That I know

But hard is good

In this case

Balance preserves the mood

Of fairness and

Considers the other too

Listening Not Fixing

Exposed to loss and tragedy

None can fix the malady

Yet listen to the sorrows

And bend ear to the sparrows

Who sing a mournful song

Of loved ones long gone.

Bad Hound

We critique what we see

That's true of ourselves.

Demanding the other

Be better than we can.

Pounding out our own evil

In our responses to others.

We pound and pound

What comes around and around.

The consuming, bad hound

That is in us.

Client's Plight is of Human

Sitting at the table,

Airing their distress.

Client's always complaining;

Trying to correct.

Wanting change of other;

Bending like hot metal,

To be a god,

In their own right.

And fashion the other,

In their image.

But human is client.

And they are us.

Acting out what we do,

But louder and louder.

So we counsel them,

To be less, like us.

To quiet the madness

That plagues humanness.

We are them and

They are us.

Choices

Decisions are derisions in the simplicity of life.

They cause upheaval and cut like a sharp knife.

But I've got it figured like an audible or blitz.

About the decisions that muddle with clean dreams.

They be obstacles with parenthetical catches

A step made, a tradeoff played, sealed in our ashes.

A Fork in the Road

A crisis of choice that I can't get around.

No one can tell which way is sound.

To choose just the one is to unchoose another.

A fork in the road: one path equal to other.

Crossing Lines

Standing with great finesse

Beside the family

Giving water glasses

To the family masses

Coming up to a bed of death

Entering upon a sacred space

A threshold where life has left

Where loved ones fear to tread

So I will lead the way

By crossing lines of fear and dread

I will lead the way

By approaching the death bed.

Boddhisatvas

Boddhisatvas enlightened; yes

Dead and returned; no

They are those who think

Beyond what we are capable.

Who connect dots with dreams;

Shedding light, casting away

Shadows upon hidden truths.

Finding the chords, the fibers

Of universal truths in the

particulars; the flowers in the

weeds; perfume in the dung heap.

Value Me

Knowing I should say what I'm feeling

But inside I'm keeping it in.

I am afraid of what you'll think

What I fear is you dismissing me

I'll show you what's important about me

But you'll not stop listening

Working my fears out with a friend

Know its helpful, but

I fear it will never end

A hopelessness takes hold and

What do I do.

Value me that's I want

I'm not a step to be skipped

Or a can to be kicked,

A stone to be thrown,

Or a booger to be flicked.

The Life You Aren't Living

All vestiges of the life you aren't living

Must go

They must go

They are an anchor

A dreadnaught carrier of scurvy and disease

A gnawing phantom limb

It must go

Live the life you are given

And make the best of it you can

The God I invented

The God we make is the one we break

We break and fashion into our own passion

He looks like us, a person plus

All our hopes and aspirations, but will look aside from our selfish
expectations

He rests above, full of love

He bends down, to receive our crown

Of approval, which he must follow or suffer removal

We placed him on the throne, just beneath our own

He is the God I invented, a God truly demented

Resembling his creatures a bit too much, corrupt and smutch

The God I invented will soon be lamented

As soon as I replace him with me

Run with it

Don't let it end this way.

Don't run with doubt too far.

Little words to make sense of

How we got here.

Don't do damage,

But run with it.

Follow it where it leads.

My Dark Passenger

My dark passenger and

Depression is his name.

He is angry and self-centered;

Always playing a dangerous game.

The world is a series of traps—

Luring you in with hope,

Capturing you with despair—

With nothing to cope.

The Water We're In

Swimming in the sea of race;

Ignoring if happening in my place—

Of work and worship

In my halls of justice.

It is the water and I a fish

Amputee

When a man cries aloud

Loudly amongst an ignoring crowd

They look away

Busy in the fray

Caught in their own dark shroud

Too busy to see

What could easily be

A man just like them

Instead they condemn

The man, an emotional amputee.

Dark Passenger Bus

We all carry with us

A friend with a fuss.

He complains

Taking great pains

On the dark passenger bus.

The passenger is really no friend

He rides without end

No leaving

Or surrendering

Giving little hope to fend.

Look You in the Eyes

I can't look you in the eyes

To do so means you're real

To look you in the eyes

Denies my unreal expectation that it will all go away

The pain between us I can't escape

My fear of you I can't mistake

It's too real to look

It's better for me that you don't exist

Ignoring the problems that can't be fixed.

Nothing Lasts

The nature's sun is shining still

The sun, the sky, the window sill

Echoes forth the sing-song wind

Carries forth the pervasive Adam sin

Gather ye and harken all

God's great wrath will cast a pall

And he who opposes shall be cut down

As the grass withers and the age of man fades

So too glory shall glory raise

Like Christ from the tomb

And Lazarus from the cave

All shall see as an age comes to pass

For nothing, even man, will ever last

Stand Firm

Burn with fires indignant as you

Pick against the scab,

Bite back at the disease

Causing your erosion.

Bore your roots ever deeper

Than where you are.

Bear them down into who you are

Bear down, down into your core.

Fight, not for what is yours, but

For who you are.

Lay down your rights when needed,

But lose sight not;

The vision of your identity.

Bend like a Reed

Fluid is the water that flows

Between wilt and rot

Fluid is the man that grows

Despite his lot

Bend as needed for life is change

Bend like a reed and welcome the strange.

The Forces that Influence your Darkness

Love and know that you are loved.

Let that be your shield and sword

Against the forces that influence your darkness.

Challenge all that is seductively revengeful;

The greatest temptation to darkness.

Love and know that you are loved

Let that be your shield and sword

Against the forces that influence your darkness

Dreams Await

Fare thee well into that soft slumber

Where horse and deer and dog float

In sky of wonder, full of starry heavens.

Billowy shadows against blue velvet dusk.

Beacons of light call out from beyond.

Leading the way through dark highways.

Passages through the sky taking you unknown.

Hope

Hope is the worst thing of all,

It's the cruelest tease,

It shatters your heart.

Hope is the best thing of all,

It makes any struggle tolerable,

It fills the heart with strength.

When Joy Ascends

Two leering lights in the fore;

Two lights I've never seen before.

Parallel pin drops of red light daggers;

Stretched across gray dark staggers.

Outreaching like a flat descending staircase.

Looking back under an elliptical phase;

Reading me like an alien gaze

Seeing me with no love or compassion.

Causing my face crestfallen and ashen.

Reminding me joy and emptiness are friends

My heart falls when my joy ascends.

Moments of Lucidity

Every night is an act of surrender

Laying down my mental arms for war against dreams

Every bark of dog gone asunder

Captures cats of mankind blunder

Words drop meaning when dreams escape

Moments of lucidity break in and out

But cockroaches rule precipitously

Landing bastions pouting before us

Dreams

Dreams of a bygone era pervade

In nightmares of today

Tomorrow casts shadows of

Hope upon a sunless ray

Eager hands outstretched

For shackles of freedom

Clinching the lock

Of fears succored numb

What are we to do? Become?

Give? And be?

Living in a world seeking to contain

What it cannot foresee

If It Doesn't Really Matter

If it doesn't really matter

What you say and what you do

What people think of you

And how you feel about them

Then why should who you are addressing

Care about what you are saying

You've defeated your position

In an effort fortify your ego

Against the sheer, inescapable

Fact that vulnerability is necessary

Vulnerability is fundamental

It is a human need like water

Shelter, food and sex

You need it, I need it

And because of that shared need

We must have community

Community is efficiency

Two or more people meeting

Each other's needs

So you how think you're logical

Who thinks he needs no one

Who doesn't care about others

And other's opinions of you

It does matter

It matters for your survival

It matters for your wellbeing

And the wellbeing of the human race

You matter

When Your Focus Misleads You

You're scared, I get that

And when you're scared, you want safety

I get that

But safety doesn't always equal right

Safety can sometimes be wrong

It's safe to blame the other person

But that doesn't mean you're right

You are so focused on them

You're blind to your own responsibility

And blindness is unsafe

Don't you see?

Your effort to be safe is making you unsafe

Open your eyes to the mirror in front of you

Face your own responsibility

Before you face the other's

False Starts and Mishaps

What is life about?

Is it about the perfect start?

Does your beginning destine your end?

Or is it about how you finish?

Regardless of what you've been through,

What mishaps have happened in your life,

You're going to refocus your life

And live the best life you can.

That's what life's about.

So have your false starts and mishaps.

Have as many as you like

Just make sure to learn from them

Just make sure you're better because of them.

Section 2: Aphorisms

Guiding Aphorisms

Dignity given to man, by man can be taken away. Dignity given to man by God can never be taken away.

Addiction breeds emotional immaturity in the user and the child.

Work is a treadmill.

We think upon the thoughts of those who have thought before us.

It's hard being told your wrong, especially when you're actually wrong.

God works in the mysterious as it appears to us.

Explanations of the mysteries of life relieve and disappoint.

We're all drawn to know what happens behind locked doors.

Lies and truth are blurred in the allusion.

Wild Aphorisms

Protest actuates the mechanism of justice.

Standing aside to injustice does not put aside one's responsibility.

To watch injustice with indifference is equal to the injustice itself.

When hurt do not respond with hurt.

Stop, drop, and listen to God.

God is present in our worst and best moments.

Women are on the up as men miss their nightly sup.

Racist and incoherent, two elements find an easy cohesion in ignorance.

We all try to control our circumstances, but the control of a person is abuse.

Sexual expression outside of a relationship is always selfish.

Sexual expression outside of relationship destroys the soul.

Aphorisms of Image

Image of God is what we are and what we are to be.

Image is to make the invisible visible, to make the God unseen seen through us.

Image is truly found in the individual, it is truly found in the whole, in man and woman.

Image is to be responsible for the created order, but not to worship it.

Image broken and resilient, yet its future fulfillment breaking in to the present.

Aphorisms for Today

The horrors done to us become the horrors we do to others.

What we take in can add, subtract, or modify, but its influence is never neutral.

The lies we tell ourselves help and hurt in so many ways; it is true humility to know the difference.

We are influenced so much by so little.

Uncritically consumed media is the plague of our nation.

Relativity applied to anything other than physics voids any veracity of any judgment; where's the self-defeating color to paint my corner?

Of celebrities and whores, what's the difference besides salaries?

Self-sabotage the safety mechanism to success.

True terror is looking into the face of someone who has lost all tethers to reality.

The most dangerous man is the one whose quest has lost all connection with reality

The heat of battle provides poor analysis of strategy.

Section 3: Short Story

Eternal Memory

Chapter I

7th period just let out and I was waiting for my mom to pick me up from school. I wanted to get home soon because practice tonight started at 7pm and I wanted to put the last touches on a new painting of children playing in a field. Painting was my new obsession. I thought about it every day, daydreamed about what I could create on the canvas in class, and wandered the halls imagining rotund figures with robotic arms and alien heads. Or giant cityscapes crowded together with angels descending on them like snowflakes ushering out a call of destruction on the citizens. These worlds and characters offered sweet relief from the pain filled reality that is high school. I craved escape from parents yelling and screaming all the time, not fitting in at school, and being the worst player on the basketball team.

My mom finally pulled up in our Toyota van, god I could have died of embarrassment. Most drives home followed a similar routine. My mom would ask me a litany of questions about my day. I would respond with one word answers wishing she would stop giving me the third degree. My mind usually wandered during the questions and I often thought about how it's strange that I used to talk to her just fine. But now, it's all I can do to string together a few syllables of coherent thought. It was becoming increasingly more difficult to open to anyone. The tortuous 17 minute car ride was over and I hopped out of the van and quickly made my way to my room closing the door behind me. I sighed with relief and plopped down on the love seat. The couch was the one clean spot in my entire room. The rest is covered in dirty clothes, paints, paint covered shirts I use as rags for my brushes, homework assignments, and half completed drawings.

I don't know if anyone else likes my paintings. But honestly, I don't really care. Each piece ushers me into another world where I can be free, where I don't have to think about the problems in my life. I could easily get lost for hours in one of my worlds, but my mom's request to come outside snapped me back into reality. Coming out of my room I see that my dad was getting home. My jaw tightened and my head dropped down. He came in the front door and hardly noticed me. My heart sunk like it did every night. I loved my family, but I couldn't fix them. I felt like I was to blame for our issues. And when I feel this way, the only that helps is to slip into my one of my worlds. I could slip into forever.

Chapter II

My dad picked me up from practice. Silence is our form of communication. He sat there not knowing how to talk to me and I, being so insecure and afraid of his anger, sat passive. We pulled up to my house. I get out and walk into the house. I heard what sounded like crying from my moms' bedroom. My parents had been fighting again. If only I could have done something. A wave of powerless anger washes over.

I push those thoughts out of my head, head to my room and pick up another project. Hours drifted by before I noticed it was time for bed. It took me awhile clear my head. Kept thinking about my family. Finally, my thoughts slow and sleep comes. My dreams aren't much better than reality. Late in the night I awoke in a cold sweat shaking. I looked around the room to orient myself. It was still dark outside and I didn't know what time it was. I closed my eyes and tried going back to sleep, but I was too stressed. I lied in the dark and looked at my paintings hanging on my bedroom wall. It was then that I heard a curious sound, it sounded like a small voice shouting.

"I can't take it anymore, he has to go!"

"It will all be okay. I'll talk to him."

"What was that?" I wondered. To my surprise, the lamp sitting on my desk twisted around and illuminated my picture of the children playing in the field. To my amazement the children leapt off the canvas and on to the wall.

I watched in delight as the children smiled and played, "Hello!" I said to them. But they didn't hear me, they just kept on playing. Then, as quickly as they came to life, they were whisked off into darkness. Astonished by the sight, I touched the wall to see if I wasn't going mad. I felt a pang of sadness, the children's going caused my heart to sink. I turned to see the lamp that sat beside my bed, it had somehow changed. It almost had a face. And didn't it just talk? Who was it talking to?

I looked at it for some time. It didn't move, but I felt like we were having an eye staring contest. I shrugged my shoulders and wrote the whole thing off as a weird side effect of my dream. I lie silently. Right as I'm about to fall asleep again, I hear the voice.

"Um excuse me, Pete." I looked back at the lamp. The once semi-face like features of the lamp now bore a rather sympathetic expression. It was unmistakable! The lamp had a face and just spoke to me.

I responded "Yes?" incredulously, humoring the ridiculousness of the situation.

"So sorry about that outburst a moment ago; you see the bookshelf and the chest of draws over there are in a bit of a tiff and I'm playing mediator" said the lamp looking apologetic. I didn't quite know how to respond. The lamp noticed my befuddlement and decided to do a bit of explaining.

"Pete I can see that you're taken aback, but I assure you these two fight quite often. There's no need to be alarmed." The lamp felt assured that his statement would put my unsettled state to rest.

"But... how... uh... what I'm trying to say..." the words couldn't get out of my mouth. I took a deep breath, collected my senses, tried again. "But how is it that I'm talking to you? You're a lamp! Lamps don't talk. Lamps aren't alive!" I exclaimed. After hearing this, the lamp wore a grave expression on his face.

He mumbled to himself "Not alive?"

The lamp thought for a moment, looked back up at me and said earnestly "I assure you Pete, I'm very much alive and so are the bookshelf, chest of draws and the others too. We're as real as you are." I always thought there was something fishy going on in my room, but never did I imagine anthropomorphic furniture.

The lamp shared that everyone in the admired me very much and loved my new obsession of painting. It was then that I remembered my painting of the children playing in the field and how they leapt off onto the wall. I grabbed the canvas off the wall and looked at it. The children were gone. It was just an empty field.

"But where did the children go? They all looked so lively and joyful!" I thought to myself and the sadness of their absence returned. For so long that picture had served as my escape from the drudgeries and pains of my existence. I wanted to know what that darkness was that enveloped them. I turned to the lamp and said innocently "Lamp, what happened to the children? They vanished from my painting!"

"Oooh... So you're curious about the waves are you?" he said with a knowing grin scuttling across his face.

"Waves?"

"Waves, that's right. Those children in the field went to a far off place. You probably saw its door. It was the darkness."

My eyes grew big with wonder. I looked out the window into the darkness lost in thought. Waves? Darkness? Door? What did it all mean?

I looked back at him from my thousand yard stare and asked him what kind of place was this other world.

He replied, "It's a place where all of life's experiences and memories are collected together into a great sea, and sometimes, you can catch sight of a wave."

My gaze drifted back to the window.

"Sounds better than living here!" I thought to myself.

The lamp must have read my thoughts because he said "I'm sure you're thinking that this is an incredible place and that you would like to go there, am I right?"

I nodded in agreement. I then said "How do you get there?"

"I knew you'd ask, but I must warn you, it is not a safe place." The lamp said with a serious expression.

"Many have gone and few have narrowly escaped. It is a place of trapped shadows and bygone souls. Only the Eternal Memory is able to exist at the center of that swirling mass."

Thankful, but his warning had little effect on me. I wanted to follow the children and see this other world. I pressed the lamp further to tell how to get there. I pleaded "Please lamp, you've always shown me the light. What do I have to do to get there?" But the lamp refused to tell me, insisting that it would be too dangerous. I begged and pleaded into the night until the lamp had no recourse, but to tell me.

"Alright, alright! If you want to know so badly I'll tell you." I was all ears.

"Don't get too excited, passage is not easy. Many have refused to go simply because the way to get there is so hard." I dropped the smile, but not my excitement. The lamp looked at me straight in my face and asked "It can be a place of healing, wonder and excitement; or one of horror, sadness and pain. It depends on what the sojourner brings in with him. It's a place where you face your true self." I pondered this for some time. The lamp was patient, but finally asked "Do you still want to go?"

I looked at him determinedly and said "Yes."

The lamp bore a serious expression. He said "The currency for entrance is one's most painful experience. To enter this world you must be willing to relive the worst day of your life."

Silence stirred for a moment. I looked again very hard and perplexed at the lamp, and if my face did not state it clearly enough, I said "What?"

The lamp explained "The door to the great sea lies in your most painful memory." I searched my memory. I asked myself

"What was my most painful memory?" It was hard to think. I've spent so much time escaping my life. I'm not even sure what my most painful memory is. Stillness sat pregnant in the room for some time, my mind was working hard. The lamp simply stared at me, studying my face. More and more time passed, I was fighting with myself. "What if I can't do this? What If I have to relive something that I don't want to relive? I'm not sure I can do this." I thought.

This was a once in a life-time offer. I couldn't let fear keep the door closed. And like that, I remembered. I took a deep breath and let the memory flood my mind. Before the first tear could leave my cheek I was gone.

Chapter III

The sun was shining. A breeze danced lightly across my cheek whisking away the tear. I found myself reposed at the base of a weeping willow in a place I had never been before, yet seemed familiar. I rose to my feet from a sitting position on a beautifully lush green lawn. Up the slight incline was a house. This place struck me as odd.

It seemed the house I was looking at was bigger than it ought, but what did I know, "Maybe that's how it's supposed to be?" I thought to myself.

It occurred to me; after the breeze stole my tear away everything around me became deathly still. The air, the sunbeams, even flies grew static. Then a voice out of nothingness took shape. At first I could not make it out. It was so faint, yet it distinctly belonged to a woman.

"A refined lady" I thought. It came out now boldly, like cascading rains upon a windshield. I began to make some of it out…

"Flowing drifts of sentiment,
Nostalgia is the recollection of the past,
Experiences that remind us of the future,
Don't cry for me weeping willow."
"That last part was almost in song" I thought.

"Curious words" I wondered about their meaning. The voice grew faint again. Looking at the strange house again, my curiosity compelled me to approach it.

I walked up the steps onto the porch and quietly through the open door. All was silent. The room was filled with a twist of silence and timelessness. The silent held a deep centralizing power much like the base of a pyramid holding the structure together, or the binding of a book keeping each page in its proper place.

Apart from the strangeness it was obvious I was in a laundry room. Socks stuffed in a shelf interspersed with laundry detergent, batteries, a few tools and other sundry household items. On the other side of the small passageway hung well-worn dress shirts hanging by small metal pegs uniformly spaced in a homemade pegboard. By the look of it, whoever lived here was poor and created what they could not afford. I moved on and made my way passed two bedrooms on either end with a bathroom near me on my right. In front of me sat a wood fire stove and a tiny kitchen. Glancing in each room it was clear that children lived here.

It was just then that I felt a slight touch; a soothing touch reminiscent of a lighthouse in a tumultuous sea of stillness. It guided me through many rooms. I stopped. The touch had left. I was where it wanted me to be. I looked around. I realized I was in a double-wide mobile home. The furniture was tattered and shabby. There were visible holes in the carpet; couches were well worn. Through the window I could see a large oak tree providing shade for a rusted metal play-set. I could see brown patches at the end of the slide and below the three swings. Across the yard was a gravel drive way. By the indentations in the gravel I could see that two cars usually park there. Odd, seeing no cars present in the driveway gave me a strange sense of relief. I turned to my left to face a door slightly opened. In it was a lone boy, noiselessly playing. He startled me. If I hadn't looked, I wouldn't have seen him. I did not move for fear of disturbing him. I simply watched; matching his silence with my own.

Chapter IV

My eyes trained on the boy. There was such innocence about him. He seemed to be the picture of purity. His skin was pale white, almost angelic. His dark black hair cut in a bowl shape. He wore a sports jersey with matching blue sweatpants and white sneakers. He sat on the floor crisscross applesauce, playing with an assortment of trains, cars and action figurines. His world was inhabited by army men desperately driving their locomotive to the other side of town to rescue a damsel in distress as the evil Tyrannosaurus Rex sped after them in a rickety old Ford truck.

Looking around his room I saw a bed, dresser and a small waste paper basket. Along the trim of the walls, close to the ceiling, were delightful stencils of blue clouds. The dresser had the same designs on them. It was a great room for a young imaginative mind to soar in the clouds and create stories and fantasies. Just then, a beam of orange and yellow light struck my eyes. Turning my head to the window I noticed the sun perched atop the horizon about to topple over like a glass of wine.

Immediately I saw the boy seize up as if his spine had been replaced with a steel rod. A dark presence grew all around him. I looked around and saw nothing, but I heard something. I heard the impenetrable lock of silence open. The unique distortion of time that so tightly held this place in a stranglehold was lifted. It was a horrifying noise, a screeching smashing pitter-patter of a grown man's footsteps outside the door. The boy then became visibly distressed. Panicked I scrambled about the room, frantic to understand.

The boy was immovable like a deer in the headlights. The footsteps had now stopped. The boy's eyes widened. A slow creak emanated from the front door and a large dark figure approached. I am hesitant to say it was a man, yet for the life of me I don't know what else to call it. The figure had a strange power. The stuffed his fear deep down. The figure slowly walked in. He slipped a look at the boy that would turn fire into ice. Step...

Step...

Step...

Step...

Step...

Squeak...

The figures eyes dropped to his left foot. He stepped on one of the boy's toys that rolled out during his play. Without provocation and reason the figure approached the boy with a quickening pace, what seemed like 15 feet turned into an arm's length. The figure's speed escalated to a maddening swiftness. The boy terrified, he froze in place. The figure lighted upon him as a father attacking the criminal who raped his daughter with indiscriminate, blind furious rage. The boy screamed followed by a muffled utterance. And then, silence...

Chapter V

I found myself cast into black raging waters. I struggled to surface and find my lungs deliverance as they screamed for air. I don't know how long the struggle lasted. What seemed like minutes turned into hours. Finally, breaching the surface, I made such a terrible noise I'm sure I scared all the stars away. The seas were dark, farther on was an ominous shroud of visibleness. The colors emanating were awe-inspiring: translucent and luminescent, bright and warm. Yet, regardless of how amazing the sight was, I still felt danger all around me.

I sensed something beyond all senses, a residual touch from that in-observable place. My fascination quickly faded by my need of self preservation. Seeing a nearby object I desperately grabbed for it. At first it seemed like a log, but after further inspection I realized it was a trunk. As I looked, I saw that it was a full tree, the weeping willow from the house, lying stationary underwater upside down. Holding on gave me a chance to catch my breath and rest for a bit. The waves died down a bit allowing me to reflect. I thought about that boy. I could not shake that look of terror in his eyes. "That poor boy! Why was no one protecting him?" I shouted. My outburst went unchallenged. No one heard my imprecation and no one answered.

Chapter VI

After resting I grew curious about the light at the center of this watery place. But curiosity was interrupted by a wave filled with paintings, finely carved sidings, beer mugs, laughing faces, legs and fire pits all rolling down on me, pushing me, back down in the depths. Like a funnel, I was directed to an enormous room. I looked around and noticed on the walls curious and quirky paintings, cartoonish posters juxtaposed next to elegant decorations. It was mishmash of styles from different eras. The color of the walls was a gay tinged green, making everything feel organic as if it were alive. The room was filled with people. They were all so comical I burst out laughing.

One piece in particular caught my attention. A moon shaped lamp, orbited by a thin clothe of turquoise hung from the ceiling. It was beautiful. It held some kind of inexplicable power, acting as a centralizing force, holding all objects and people in place.

I made my way to what seemed like an endless line of people sitting, eating and talking. They were jovial and gregarious, celebrating a great occasion. My eye caught sight of a lone silhouette far off. I looked in that direction intently, but could not make it out. Resolved to find this curiosity I crusaded about, causing all kinds of ruckus and disruption to the party goers. Searching uselessly I sat down again in a chair trying to appear inconspicuous. I couldn't enjoy the ambiance and free-spirited mood. Something compelled me to search out that silhouette. Just then, I felt eyes on me. She had been looking at me for some time now, making a careful study of my features and gestures. Determined not to be too aggressive and scare her off again, I looked back with slightly out of the corner of my eye.

Then, to my frustration, I lost sight of the mysterious figure a second time. I looked around the crowded room with no luck.

"If I had only been more direct with my looks, or if I only … ah what's the use!" I frustratedly said to myself.

A soft and sweet sound slid down my ears interrupting my sulk "Hi, I was wondering if you would want to come walk with me, that is, if you want?"

This was not merely a figure, but a beautiful young woman. I smiled. My heart was racing and my chest tight with nervous joy. I managed to say "Yes, I would like that."

We compulsively and instinctively walked side by side. Thoughts and ideas flowed freely between us. We shared a spiritual bond, one that traversed beyond the limitations of our mortal coils. Our spirits linked at first touch. From then on we did not speak a single word to each other. We didn't need words. All speech was communicated through spiritual means. Our thoughts were one and our joys were unified. The bond created a mutual strengthening and sharpening, the morphing of our beings catalyzed dormant strengths, healings, joys, hopes, dreams and vitalities into action. The connection of our spirits ignited transformation. I stopped and looked back at the moon shaped lamp hanging down from the ceiling. Its turquoise hue reassured me. The hue grew and grew. Its light enveloped me, surrounding me with a setting. I was again, in a different place.

Chapter VII

Splash! Muffled sounds of the tumultuous sea reverberated in my eardrums as I attempted to orient myself. Emerging from a fugue my consciousness returned- I precipitously grabbed a swiftly passing floating object. I was back, and, strangely now the sea had taken a different mood. Where colors were foreboding and ominous before it now resembled something friendly and inviting, so much so that my first impulse was to relax, all I wanted was to just be. Looking around I cannot justifiably describe my profound confusion over the fact that there was no sun in this place. The light reminded me of a sunset, yet it didn't emanate from the horizon in the west but from the center. Things were becoming more like as I approached the center. I felt power emitted like magnetic concentric energies pulsating in cascading motion. This energy breathed into all fiber and indivisible space around me, filling it with life.

Chapter VIII

A current pushed me forward. The sea grew pale in contrast to the awe-inspiring light just ahead of me. It dominated the area, overpowering all colors and waves, demanding my attention. Waves passed by me now, faster and faster. I could see each one was made up of my memories.

I thought "How is it that my memories are being transformed into waves? Am I in my own consciousness? Has my past become physicalized? It can't be though. This is a real, physical place. It doesn't feel like my head."

Before I knew it the waters began to overtake me. Wave after wave struck my waterlogged body. Visions of scenes crashed against me: faces, places, a host of things unfamiliar, phasing in and out of my consciousness. Some visions lasting for a considerable amount of time others were gone in a flash. They were hitting with such frequency I couldn't keep track. Rolling ahead was a wave so large it dwarfed all the other ones. It toppled onto me forcing me down. Down I went with great speed.

I hit the floor of a ram shackled room with a thud. I shakily stood up. Without decision I grabbed a rubber band next to me and wrapped it around my bicep. What was I doing? I had the crazed hunger in me. I licked my lips. Eagerly I prepared a needle to put in my last remaining "good" vein. The cool effortless slide of the plunger forced each liquid millimeter into my blood stream. Relief, sweet relief! My eyes rolled to the back of my head. A rush flooded my body, satisfying the hunger. This hit brought me back, back to that feeling of normal.

Just then, my body torpedoed out of the water, expelling me from the room like vomit out of a sick dog. The wave rolled past. I sunk into the wave's lull that it left behind. The swaying reminded me of being in a cradle. But there was no time to recover. I could see another wave hastily rumbling toward me, pulling the waters toward it. I tried to out maneuver it, but the struggle was pointless.

I was transported to a poor looking home. The wall paper looked like wood. The chairs were distressed. I thought to myself whose eyes am I going to be looking through this time? My perspective seemed off. I estimated I was just over three feet tall. Looking down I could see that I was wearing a white dress with pink poke-a-dot apron over it.

My ponytail struck my eyes as I whipped my head back to the kitchen. Horror and fear overcame me. Daddy approached mommy with a look I have never seen on anyone's face. I clutched the bottom of my skirt and yelled, "What's going on?" I cried out in fear and confusion! Why was daddy acting so strange toward mommy? Mommy was so scared. As Daddy approached mommy, he deftly snatched up a knife and raised it over his head. Mommy screamed out in terror, throwing her arms up in an attempt to protect herself. The knife plunged into Mommy's right shoulder near the clavicle. It sounded like someone hitting water with a baseball bat followed by sounds of successive crunches.

Daddy forcibly drove the knife into Mommy's chest two more times. Mommy screamed sorrowful cries. I cringed in pain for her. Minutes later, daddy stopped and walked into the kitchen. Mommy only let out a wimpish quiet sob. The life slowly oozed out of body.

There I stood. Frozen, my eyes fixed on the protruding knife standing tall like a monument in my Mommy's chest. Daddy walked back. His eyes filled with fire. I wanted to run, to scream, to tear off my skin, anything to get away. But I could not move one muscle fiber, not one strand of nerves would obey. The fear fused all my bones together and stapled my feet to the floor. I was a pillar of salt, yet my Sodom and Gomorrah didn't lie as a city behind, but as my Daddy in front. What could I do? Where could I run? A partial grin slid across my Daddy's face as he looked at her, my Daddy was happy.

Chapter IX

A dark mist emanated through the floorboards. The room was enveloped and I was transported back to the sea. The waters were filled with shadowy figures and ghoulish phantoms dancing in and out of the vastness. My confusion quickly turned to panic. The mist was so thick now it was like sea above. The sensation of sinking overwhelmed me, but I was not drowning. And as soon as the mist flooded in around me it dissipated, when it cleared, to my surprise I found myself on dry land.

I stood atop a high precipice looking out across a great kingdom. As I was taking in the vista a man approached from behind. His soft speech alerted caught me off guard. He was a beautiful creature. Instantly I was enraptured by his company. Each turn of his head and gesture of his hand was seductive. His skin was soft glowing with a pallid glimmer. Looking into his eyes I lost all awareness, they were baby blue with glints of white and reflective pthalo. He wore a loose fitting garb spackled with diamonds. A relaxed belt draped across his waist which kept the garb from tossing side to side in the hot breeze coming from the east. He seemed angelic. My ears perked up as he said,

"Man's collective eternal soul is all potent and I am His prophet.

My prophetic purpose is of desolation, indicting not only myself, but all of mankind for our overtures toward evil.

Draw near and sit, for my tale is of man's becoming."

I didn't know what to make of that, but I sat in quiet submission to this man. He gave every appearance of being a great sage.

Resting his head on his hand and folding the other arm under his elbow, he looked far off into the distance as if recounting an old memory

"Swirls of unsuppressed motivations and vagaries swept through the porous landscape of nothingness.

Uncontained thoughts created mangled manikins entangled in the elements of pomp and mire.

The enigma strained and twisted to conform it all into thingness, to personness.

But the many attempts did not match the sought desire."

His words were so marvelous and confusing. I hoped he could help explain what I had been experiencing: the memories, the sea, the great light, the waves. The man saw the look on my face and told me everything was going to be alright. It was the Eternal Memory that had brought me here. The Eternal Memory was the source of all. He was God, but not the only God. In fact, anyone can become a God. He himself was in the process of becoming God. He shared with me the way he was going to do this was to share a new truth; one better than the Eternal Memory's, which was old and archaic. It was all about love and goodness. But that's not what people wanted. People want strength, power and self-determination. And he was going to give it to them.

"Man's collective potence" he said "discovered its perfect Genesis in multiplicity.

For fragmentation to be accomplished the *eternal* soul needed first to breath in the life breathe.

The contents of this breathe was reason and power, decisiveness and self, knowledge. Not compassion, justice and mercy.

A unified inhale of what may be."

The man said this as he clenched his jaw. He shifted his sitting position, looked up at nothing in general and labored on.

"The Eternal Memory exhaled and its elements indwelt and created all.

The collective took in all possibilities, unknowns and potentialities.

The very breathe held within its limits deep ravines of joy, which we mined for exploitation.

We flooded the vacuum and had only that single breath to survive on.

We poisoned ourselves and progeny on a false truth.

I bring a better truth."

The man wrapped his arms around his torso as if protect himself.

"Love is unbecoming to me through my long journey in this world.

I am mankind's true desire borne out over past and present."

Rising to his feet he lifted his hands and with exalted voice stated,

"This new truth is reminiscent of all of mankind's wishes.

Within my bones I contain man's true evolution.

I am mankind's self-created future.

I am."

Lowering his hands and holding them together as if to offer me friendly tidings he said,

"We are cosmic freedom fighters, you and I, fighting against the inherent order.

I sing the songs of man's unrepentence to the old, oppressive system.

Within me is man's collective hope.

Beneath my flesh is the anatomy of destruction.

Calamity must come in order for the future to arise.

Our endless struggle returns like a revolving pistol chamber."

His words began to change in tone and intention. I didn't like it. It seemed as if he were trying to pull me into something. His gaze into my eyes was unbreakable. I wanted to stop looking at him, but I couldn't. He went on,

> "Oscillating devices that facilitate barbarity we hang around our necks like adorned jewelry.
>
> We turn to our inner demons while forsaking our saintly opportunities.
>
> Rationality must become insanity in order to buck the system.
>
> Follow me.
>
> Free yourself with my help."

When he finished speaking, his words caused in me such a terrible reaction. I felt nauseous. What he said unmasked his slick façade and exposed him for a devil. I see now that his beauty was not beauty at all, but beauty distorted, disfigured into a facsimile. I wanted to run away so badly, but he blocked my escape, the only exit lay before me, the precipice. Not knowing what to do I stood frozen with fear. The devil screeched. Before I knew it the man had transformed into a suffering writhing miserable creature, tortured by unseen forces. I could feel his suffering. He suffered for he did not have power, not because he was in pain. I felt strangely compassionate. I reached out to comfort him. A moment's hesitation, he looked confused and then thankful. I felt at ease and walked closer to him. With lightning speed he ripped my arm clean off my body. Blood sprayed out my delimbed torso. I clumsily staggered backwards in a stupor of trauma. I was losing my balance falling back, farther and farther towards the edge of the precipice. The pain was so intense. My right heel went back only to find nothing to support my weight. And I fell helplessly backward.

Chapter X

The fall resurfaced me in the sea. I grabbed at my arm. I had both limbs safely attached to my body. I cried out in relief. It wasn't very long before the waves picked up again. But they seemed different. They no longer seemed like memories, but more like language undulating out from the Eternal Memory like a ripple spreading out across a pond. The Eternal Memory, I now understand had been speaking to me this entire time. This confused me. What I saw, felt, and heard were the experiences of other people. How could they have been the utterances from such a being? Who, in my mind, is entirely different than anything I've encountered. The Eternal Memory was reality within reality.

I could see a mass as I was carried by a wave. I reached out and grabbed a boulder. Able to pull myself up I turned around and was dumbfounded to see above the waters. I was close to the center what the light was coming from. I could also see that the waves were flowing from the center in harmony. What seemed to be random waves trying to trample me underfoot were all concerted ripples pulsating forth from the Eternal Memory; bending and willing them into majestic forms and shapes; each emanation more intricate and beautiful then the next. All intertwining, each with its own hue and synchronized and coalescing. The waves had sound that tasted like nectar sampled from a flower off an island in the sun. Wafts of fresh smelling air took shape in front my eyes and danced across the horizon like two ballerinas skillfully prancing on a dimly lit stage. It seemed that all my senses were comingling; one playing with another like school children during recess. My senses were syncretizing into a wholly new experience.

Chapter XI

The glory that I saw made me feel unworthy. I felt shame. A figure like a man embraced my shoulders. My skin tingled, each hair stood on end. The being turned me round, yet I couldn't look at him. He touched my face and opened my eyes. His face was plain, no praiseworthy features to distinguish Him. He was at the same time an ordinary man, but not ordinary.

I looked at the figure as the tears dried and asked "Who are you?"

He responded, "You still don't know who I AM my son?" looking at me with such tenderness in His face he said, "That first experience still binds you."

"Take heed to what I have to say," he said. "The seed was sown among the thorns, this is the man who hears the word, and the worry of the world and the deceitfulness of wealth choke the word, and it becomes unfruitful."

His sternness now softened to sympathy. He then asked, "My son, can you still not trust me? I am here with you and always have been."

I heard his words. I felt his gentleness salve my broken heart, but I still could not believe that he was worthy of my trust. He could not take away my anger that I felt when seeing the boy brutalized, that poor sad boy! Where was he in that silent home? Where was when the drug addict plunged the heroin filled needle into his arm? Where was he when the little girl saw her father kill her mother? Where was he when I was being tempted by the devil? Where was he?

I said to Him with a trembling voice, "I was searching for you. I wanted to trust. I tried over and over again and with each attempt I was met with silence and abandon! And you show me all these memories, but in each one you were absent."

Maybe that devil was right. Maybe the order needs to be overturned. I shouted at him "You don't know what I went through. You don't know how desperate I was for you! Every time I thought you were near my hopes were raised only to be dashed against jagged rocks of reality."

The tears were uncontrollable now. The man looked at me like he knew exactly what I was thinking,

He said to me, "But my son, I was there. That strangeness, that otherness at the very bottom of each experience was me. Every tear trickling down your sad face, every pang of depression I was there, guiding and comforting. You allowed worry to choke out my presence, but I was there. You must have noticed that in each experience, regardless of how happy or sad or violent, that sense, that strange undeniable feeling of something greater present. That presence was my presence that was me!"

My eyes grew big again. I wanted to fight his words. I couldn't deny the loving presence in spite of the pain. His words, finally, joyfully, broke me. Some wall in my inner self crumbled; my Alamo against God. I think all along I was hoping to be defeated by Him, for only a battle could have gotten through to me.

A burst of tears, joy, laughter, sense of home, belonging, ecstasy, peace, and contentment all at once rushed in me. I felt loved. From all around came a host of voices saying…

"Out of the concerted storm
Out of the undetermined form
Out of the pain
Out of the blazen wind,
And hurried rain.

Out of the swirling trap
Out of the looming madness
Out of thunderclap,
And the black piercing sadness.

Out of the lightning trails
Out of the intense gales,
And falling nails.

Out of the menacing figures
And the ominous night creatures.

Out of the quickly formed puddle,
And mixed muddle.

Out of the soaked leaves,
Sinking from the swaying trees.

Out of the subtle movements,
And the torrential down pour.
Out of the shifting light arrangements,
And intercepted beams from the moon door.

The stillness does not come

Out of the deafening fall,
Pounding upon my eardrum.

Out of each drop of water,
Out of each glint of light,
And the unwavering falter.

Out of the unsettled
Out of the untame.
Out of the Water that burned,
              And the unpeaceful flame.
Out of the cascading
Life giving,
        Life taking,
Power!
Fire not withstanding
No dry object could long-suffer

Out of the immense kings
That mother brings,
Giving birth to life
              and strife,
From her womb we arise
              and meet our demise.

Oaks break
Dams crash
Towns destroyed
Coasts awash

Out of the bleeding heaven,
Descending clear droplets of blood.

      Comes…

            a…

            Still,

                  Unshakable…

Voice.

A pin-light to the blind
A note to the deaf kind
An idea to the dumb mind
A touch for those who search and cannot find

A voice so faint and yet so certain.
A voice trapped behind the Temple's curtain.

Be still, my son."
The voice said.

Chapter XII

And as quickly as I entered the other world I returned to my bedroom. It was still night and I was still in bed. The experience seemed too good to be true and yet, I know, I will never be the same. Not a day will go by that my life will not be influenced by this one night. As I close my eyes to sleep, I could hear the soft woman's voice sing:

"Oh lonely and starry night

Offering cool sweet breezes of soft hues

Calling out with your dim streaming light

Dark sinews reaching forth

Streaming down like a spiders webs

Calling, calling out to true north

Melting dusk, trickling down to the horizon

Candescent drops drip as if the sky was a frozen waterfall

Casting shadows over the sky like a face wizened

Bathed in the moonlight

The heavens clothed in black shadows of dark blue

Rippling pure light."

About the Author

Daniel Bates is a Licensed Mental Health Counselor who works with families dealing with violence, substance abuse and legal issues. He loves to write, think critically and drink coffee. He's passionate about writing and reading poetry, discussing philosophy/theology, spending time with his wife and daughters, connecting with friends and getting lost in a good book. He's fascinated by the intersection of faith/spirituality and mental health. He's written three books of poetry, a nonfiction book on the Christian mystics, and a self-help book on how to use the lessons life teaches us which are available on Amazon in Kindle and paperback. Daniel also writes for two online magazines: mum.info and FamilyShare.com in addition to his own blog. You can find links to Daniel's books, read his blog, and view and purchase his paintings at his website danielbates.co.

More from Daniel Bates

The Modern Mystic

Wish your spiritual life wasn't mediocre? Is your prayer life dead? Are you jealous of the spiritual vitality that everyone else seems to have except for you? Don't let your life be ruled by a spiritual malaise. Instead of checking out, go further and deeper in to the heart of God.

But how?

The Christian mystics are ancient voices with a modern message. They teach that the love of God is deeper, wider and beyond anything you can understand. It is altogether mysterious and right in front of you. It is the paradoxical truth wrapped in the unimaginable love of a relational God eager to know and be known by you.

Yes, you are the object of God's love. And yes, God is the ultimate source of your happiness. Knowing and experiencing God's love will change you. Yet experiencing God's love is not a destination. It is a journey. And you are a sojourner in need of a guide. Allow the Christian mystics to direct you along the sometimes confusing wandering path of God's love.

When Parenting Backfires

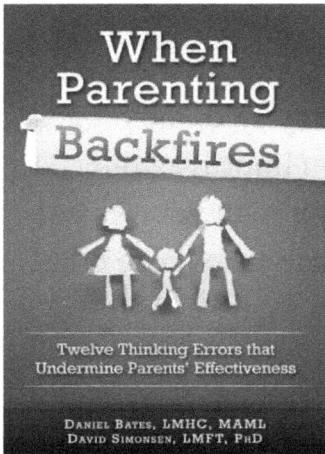

Let's be honest. Parenting is hard. From the moment children take their first breaths, parents are faced with decisions and choices that no manual could ever fully explain. And the way you parent is constantly changing: babies need protection, toddlers need direction, and teens need influence. We as parents are simply expected to do it and do it well.

From two therapists who have a combined 25 years of experience working with families comes a new kind of parenting book. This book doesn't focus on technique, a discipline scheme or parenting style. This book focuses on the parent themselves, specifically the kind of thinking that makes parents effective or ineffective. In *When Parenting Backfires* examines 12 thinking errors commonly made by parents. In each chapter Dan and David:

- Explain the thinking error
- How it backfires
- What parents can do to correct the thinking error

- And real life examples of parents who have recognized their thinking error, made the correction, and improved their effectiveness.

Let this book do its work. Let down your guard and be open to the new ideas. As I've already said, the biggest risk you'll take is to your ego as you improve your parenting skills and your relationship with your kids. I think any effective parent is willing to take those odds. Are you?

Learning to Live

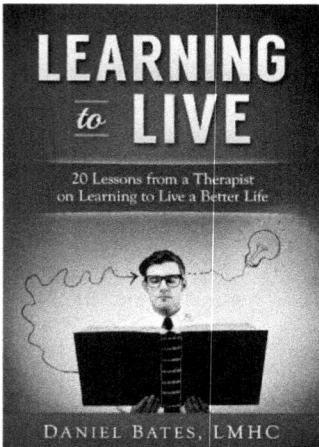

You are the reason you are stuck.

You can either stay stuck or learn how to get un-stuck. In order to get un-stuck, you must engage in the learning process. That means learning about yourself, your perceptions, your thinking, your communication style, and how you view relationships. But learning is hard to do with some help. Fortunately, an experienced therapist, Daniel Bates, has compiled 20 lessons based on his clinical experience and the latest social science research to help you.

Learning to Live will help you engage with the lifelong work of learning. Learning isn't an event, it's a journey.

It can be painful, challenging at times and downright uncomfortable, but the end result is worth it. Lessons have a way of sticking with you for the rest of your life. They are the gift that keeps on giving. So, what are you waiting for? Start learning so you can start living.

Mental Health Taxes

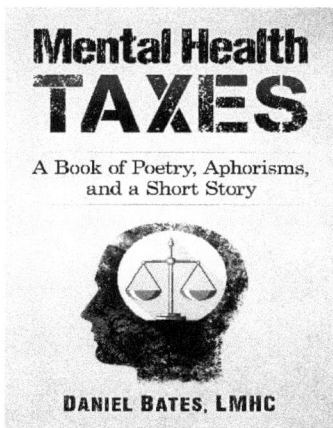

Poetry is an act of contrition. It's the art of looking at life in a painfully honest way. Poetry uses metaphors to capture life's intricate complications where plain, obvious and straightforward language fails.

This book explores those metaphors like the tax collector. Your difficult relationship is like an invisible tax collector on your mental health. Your stress is a mental health collector. Your fear of engaging with loss, pain, addiction, denial is your tax collector and it will keep collecting and collecting. Your mental health is taxed by what you avoid.

This is a work of art with the hidden agenda of helping you, art is subversive like that. Art without a purpose is just noise. The subversive purpose of this book is for you to engage with what you are most afraid to face.

Embrace the discomfort. Become what life is shaping you into. Enjoy!

False Starts and Mishaps

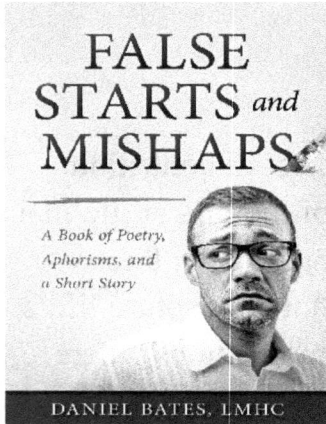

Life is full of false starts and mishaps. But what's so great about how you start? Why do people care so much about where you come from, your family, what school you went to, do you have money? Shouldn't the focus be on how you use what you have?

And what's the deal with mishaps in life? A friend moves away, you lose your job, your kids don't respect you, loved one dies? Why do those things have to derail your life? These questions and more are explored in False Starts and Mishaps.

But isn't this a book of poetry? Shouldn't the book be about nature and flowers and babies or something? Poetry has a subversive agenda of trying to help with beautiful words, images and metaphors.

Podcasts and Blog from Daniel

Brainchild is a podcast for those who want to be entertained and informed. Brainchild goes deep into the latest research from psychology, the insights from counseling, and the personal experiences Daniel has accrued over his career. You can find Brainchild at brainchildpodcast.co on Podbean. You can also listen to Brainchild on Daniels' website, danielbates.co, and find blogs, books and more.

Daniel co-hosts a podcast with author and therapist David Simonsen, PhD. The podcast focuses on mental health, relational and emotional growth, and pop culture. Dan and David take calls from listeners with relational and mental health questions, they interview special guests, review movies and analyze the political landscape through the lens of a therapist.

Daniel Bates
1000 by 30

Daniel's blog, videos, books, and information about counseling services can be found on his website, danielbates.co. In addition to his self-help material, you can learn more about Daniel's artistic interests. He's written three books of poetry and loves to paint. His poetry and paintings are featured on the website.

Counseling Services

LACAMAS
COUNSELING

If you are interested contacting Daniel for counseling, he recently expanded his private practice at Lacamas Counseling in Camas, Washington. You can find information about Daniel's counseling specialties, location of the office or other counselors that may be a fit for you at lacamascounseling.com. He's currently accepting new clients. Email or Call to schedule an appointment.